M. Powell
0208 533 663_
07930 536 62_

D0943369

singles 707

volume three

37 ways to recognise your life partner
43 truths about divorce and re-marriage
36 questions before you say 'I do'
& more

© 2001 Matthew Ashimolowo

Published by Mattyson Media an imprint of MAMM
Matthew Ashimolowo Media Ministries
57 Waterden Road
Hackney Wick
London
E15 2EE

ISBN 1 874 646 47 3

All rights reserved. No part of this
publication may be reproduced, stored in a retrieval system, or be
transmitted, in any form, or by any means, mechanical,
electronic, photocopying or otherwise
without prior written consent of the
publisher.

Bible quotes are from the King James Bible
unless otherwise stated as the following:

contents

61 truths about covenant men and covenant women

1. Godly wise men avoid the trap of comparing their partners to their mother or sister.

The role of the wife and a mother of children and supporter of husband is enough for a woman. To try to make a personal mother or sister out of her is too much a demand. It is important for a man to know precisely what he wants, and make it known to his future spouse, before he says 'I do'.

2. Godly wise men do not do the comparing thing.

A godly man will recognise the uniqueness of the person he is in relationship with. God does not produce duplicates, God wants us to celebrate our differences and not be offended by it.

3. Godly wise men are:

- Real - they refuse to walk in what they are not.
- Fruitful - They are productive
- Multiply - raising the productivity of all those around them
- Replenish - they raise the next generation and impact them positively
- Subdue - they are in charge of their environment and not vice versa.

4. Dropping your name and taking the name of your husband, is one of the steps in the covenant of marriage and it means you are taking on the destiny of the man.

5. Wise men do not impress women with their dreams, goals, and visions if they have no marriage intentions.

6. Godly wise men are frank about their health and finances.

The man who is frank enough to reveal his health or financial need is not weak, but has demonstrated strength by choosing to be vulnerable to a person whom he will share the future with.

And they were both naked, the man and his wife, and were not ashamed.
Genesis 2:25 (KJV)

7. The devil is afraid of the male seed and does everything he can to destroy the male seed.

8. Women do not quite get their satisfaction from their work. They normally get it from themselves or from their husbands when they get married.

9. Multiply - Raise the productivity of others around you. If you are a man nobody should hang around you and not improve.

10. God made the man to be special so there is no reason to carry yourself with low self-esteem.

11. Even if you do not have a job you are still God's best shot.

Men validate themselves by the job they do and the title they carry. It is important to establish your worth in God without the presence of these things.

12. Replenish - Leave a deposit for the next generation, influence youngsters. Give, reproduce after your kind.

13. A man needs to answer questions such as: Am I adding value or trouble daily by my lifestyle?

14. Reproduce your faith in your children through your gifting and ability.

15. You are ordained by God to operate in dominion. Take charge of your environment.

16. Men have to take responsibility for their environment and in this area, failure is a response you permit.

17. A Godly man has to choose to live right in the midst of the visual attack on our society.

18. Godly wise men are not carried away by looks though looks are important.

19. Godly and wise men do not let television or society dictate how they live.

Brethren, be not children in understanding: howbeit in malice be ye
children, but in understanding be men.
1 Corinthians 14:20 (KJV)

20. Godly wise men do not pick broken girls. You have to be wholesome first before you make a choice.

21. Godly men avoid demanding to touch, to taste & to test.

- You have got to treat her as God's temple, God's princess.
- If you know there are some environments you cannot control, stay away.
- Wise men are also careful in the use of the phrase " I love You"

  Love for a woman is a wholesome thing, for a man, it is one more thing in the box.

22. Protects a woman sexually by not taking advantage.

There are unsaved men who carry themselves in honour and will not take advantage of a woman sexually. If the unsaved can do it, the believer should much more be able since, he has the power of the Holy Spirit to help him.

Then he answered and spake unto me, saying, This is the word of the LORD unto Zerubbabel, saying, Not by might, nor by power, but by my spirit, saith the LORD of hosts.
Zechariah 4:6 (KJV)

23. Focuses on a woman's internal beauty.

Men by nature are visual, and therefore do not need to deny their appreciation of the beauty of the person they intend to share the future with. But it is important to also focus on internal quality, because the inner qualities to a lot of extent will determine if you have found the person who will be able to handle life's challenges with you.

24. Is able to control his emotions.

Our society measures men by how they look. Physically they look like Adonis or Arnold Schwarzzerneger, and yet the same persons have not been able to manage their anger. No matter how handsome and physically built a man is, the Bible still says:

> Be not hasty in thy spirit to be angry: for anger resteth in the
> bosom of fools.
> Ecclesiastes 7:9 (KJV)

25. Protects a woman's emotions.

Boaz was brave enough to ensure that Ruth was never embarrassed or emotionally abused whilst she was in his care. He rather spoke for her so that she was not without protection.

26. Is cautious and aware of the woman's need.

Being insensitive is an easy trap for men to fall into. From the way they manage their dating to how relationships take place within the matrimonial home. The nature of men which aids their quick arrival at satisfaction and their desire to go on to the next matter, brings them into opposition with the woman who is very opposite. The woman takes her time before she finds fulfilment emotionally in activities that are having to do with the opposite sex. The godly wise man makes effort to be aware of the woman's need.

27. Tolerant of imperfections.

A godly man waits for mistakes to turn to miracles. He is not unaware of the challenges a woman faces and the imperfections which he sees, and yet, in wisdom he praises such a woman.

28. Others-centered, meek.

Look not every man on his own things, but every man also on the things of others.
Philippians 2:4 (KJV)

29. Teachable, open minded.

A bishop then must be blameless, the husband of one wife, vigilant, sober, of good behaviour, given to hospitality, apt to teach;
1 Timothy 3:2 (KJV)

30. He pursues excellence and wants to please God.

Forasmuch as an excellent spirit, and knowledge, and understanding, interpreting of dreams, and shewing of hard sentences, and dissolving of doubts, were found in the same Daniel, whom the king named Belteshazzar: now let Daniel be called, and he will shew the interpretation.
Daniel 5:12 (KJV)

Then this Daniel was preferred above the presidents and princes, because an excellent spirit was in him; and the king thought to set him over the whole realm.
Daniel 6:3 (KJV)

31. A man of integrity, he keeps his word.

But above all things, my brethren, swear not, neither by heaven, neither by the earth, neither by any other oath: but let your yea be yea; and your nay, nay; lest ye fall into condemnation.

James 5:12 (KJV)

A man is only as good as his word is. If your word is bad, you are bad. God is good because His Word is good. God's Word is also good because He is good. The quality of the fulfilment of your promises, is a mirror of the quality of your inner life.

32. They are marked by their ability to keep their promise or their word. Stand by your word.

33. They allow the Lord to lead them into His favour.

For as many as are led by the Spirit of God, they are the sons of God.
Romans 8:14 (KJV)

So the LORD alone did lead him, and there was no strange god
with him.
Deuteronomy 32:12 (KJV)

34. If you lead yourself, you may lead yourself wrong.

So the LORD alone did lead him, and there was no strange god
with him.
Deuteronomy 32:12 (KJV)

Jesus' departure to the wilderness to wait on God in fasting and praying was by the leading of the Holy Spirit.

THE COMPROMISING MAN
35. Exploits a woman sexually.

The story which comes to mind is that of Amnon, the son of David, who deceived Tamar, his half-sister, because he wanted to exploit her sexually, and hated her more, after using and abusing her.

36. Focuses on the woman's external beauty or quality.

The comments of Samson to his parents, as to his desire to marry Delilah, gives the impression that her external beauty delighted him. Not the inner quality and the contribution she was going to make to the fulfillment of his destiny and purpose.

37. Are controlled by their emotions - lust or anger.

Samson was a strong and weak man. Strong to pull down strongholds, fight a hundred men, but weak in managing his lust and his anger.

38. Ruins a woman's reputation.

The end result of Amnon's desire towards Tamar was to take away her virginity, ruin her reputation, break her heart, and cause family difficulties.

39. They are angry when they do not get their own way.

Esau compromised and sold his birthright for a pot of one night's meal, and yet got angry because he could not get his own way.

40. They do not notice or care about the woman's need.

Compromised men would only use a woman, and even in marriage, sex is what a woman is made for, to satisfy the urge of the man and when his desires are satisfied, he rolls over and starts snoring.

41. They are critical and intolerant of any woman.

No woman is good enough for the compromised man. He has a 'but' against each one and is intolerant of all of them. But he is like Jonah, who blames everyone but himself. And when everyone repented, he did not. God repented that he wanted to destroy Nineveh, Nineveh repented, the men in the ship repented, but Jonah refused to change.

42. Control freak.

Compromised men are control freaks who want things set in certain ways. Living with them or moving around them has to be a maneuver you negotiate all the time.

43. Self-centered.

The world oscillates around the compromised man, he must be noticed, he must be satisfied. When the attention is off him, he becomes critical and angry.

44. Rigid, he thinks he knows all things.

The compromised man does not want to be seen to be wrong. He knows all things, he can do all things, and even where he is wrong, he finds a nice way to justify his stand.

45. Always have excuses for not doing things well.

The compromised man blames the sun for not shining, his parents for not paying his school fees, the flower delivery man for not bringing the flowers which he should take to his girlfriend. There is always somebody who did not do the right thing, except him.

46. He lacks integrity and honour.

Integrity and honour are watchwords of people who want to please God, who want to be unflinching in their commitment. The same quality is brought into relating to a woman, they pursue and relate with integrity and honour. But the compromised man would not, he sees this too as a price too high to pay to keep the trust of a woman. The irony of it, is that the compromised man does not show integrity and honour to others also.

THE COVENANT WOMAN

47. Relates to men who honour God with their substance. If they do not give to God, they will not give to you.

48. They are not into unwise submission. If you have to earn the love that is abuse.

49. Dressing shows decorum, shows strength and makes you attractive.

50. To be attractive and not to draw attention, is what pleases God!

The woman who get attention by the dresses she wears, will very soon discover that needle and thread can only hold her for a short while.

51. Godly wise women do not walk in self-pity.

Calling a 'pity-party' is what a godly woman would choose to not walk in, but grow away from. Because in order to be a successful woman behind a successful man, she has got to realise that when he is down, her self-pity will not pull him up. It takes those who are up, to pull the down up.

52. People with low self-esteem sell themselves to whoever is available.

The woman who is raised in the atmosphere where her self-esteem has been battered, taken away from her and torn in pieces, would turn to anyone who gives her the impression that she is loved, even if it is for ulterior motives. The highest level of pregnancies out of wedlock is among people with the lowest self-esteem.

53. "If you kiss a toad, you will come back with slime on your face." It is a fairytale that you will kiss a toad and it will change into Prince Charming.

Do not live in an illusionary world. A godly wise woman knows that she must honestly and critically analyse a proposal; a relationship, and draw her conclusions if it is the one that would hurt or help her.

54. Yesterday's hurt should not mean today's cowardice.

The nature of a woman to remember and keep things for long has made a lot of people to be trapped. So that they are busy romancing yesterday's hurt and missing today's opportunities. A godly woman would recognise that yesterday is gone, and today is slipping by. Whatever you put in store today will be delivered to you in the future.

55. Develop self-respect - Accept who you are.

In spite of the troubles which life deals out to a person, their self-respect must not be taken from them. It is one asset that can recover every other lost asset.

56. If you were the one pursuing, you would have to maintain the marriage.

As hard as it is for many young ladies who are seeking to be married, and particularly for those who are older singles, it is important to not pursue a man, but to wait to be pursued - for the man to be the giver and you to be the receiver. For him to be the hunter and you to be the hunted. If it is turned around in the opposite way, it will become an abomination, and also become a picture of how your marriage will be. You would maintain the marriage, while he sees himself as loafing.

57. Avoid having babies for the wrong reasons.

What has a single lady got to do with having babies anyway!
It is important for you to recognise that purity pays. What you
compromise to get, you would also lose. Keep yourself pure.

58. There is nothing like accidental pregnancy. Never allow the enemy to lie to you.

59. There is nothing like safe sex - 'no sex please, I am a godly woman'.

The United Nations along with the nations of the earth have been peddling the practice of safe sex. It is on the television in every country you go, in almost all the languages. Safe sex by the world's standard is not 'No sex', but having sex using a condom. It is important for us to understand that it is not a game, it is a sacred act which binds two people in covenant together. If you have no covenant with that man, as in marriage, you are not supposed to be in any copulation.

60. It will be the lowest of the lowest self-esteemed woman who will use a pregnancy to force a commitment.

61. Godly wise women have an eye for protectors.

One of the chief functions of a man is to be the protector. The wisdom of a woman will be revealed in her ability to detect who will protect her, and bring herself under his covering. Jesus said "A man should love a woman, as Christ loved the church". One of the chief functions of Christ is to protect His church. The man also will serve as protection for the woman.

42
truths
about
cross-
cultural
marriages

62. Family expectations can affect the couples' growth and independence i.e. Involvement of the family in their affairs, family traditions.

63. Understanding each other's cultural background will help the marriage to succeed.

64. Respecting the differences in each other's culture, in particular the key important aspects, will ensure a healthy appreciation of one another.

65. Language barriers may occur and need to be worked on to ensure good communication and understanding between the couple.

66. Imposing cultural values on your partner will add unwarranted pressures.

67. Disregarding cultural values that are held dearly by your spouse will be a source of conflict if not addressed and understood prior to marriage.

68. More time at the pre-marital stage should be spent on a couple who are entering into a cross-cultural marriage.

69. Mindsets may differ due to the level of exposure to the culture or limited experience to other cultures.

70. Eating habits should not be overlooked. One of the ways to a man's heart is through his stomach.

71. Children born into the relationship should be given an understanding of the culture of both parents.

72. Unhealthy competition between cultures should be avoided. One is not more supreme than the other.

73. Involvement of friends in imposing their values and expectations on the spouse can bring pressure on the relationship.

74. How a spouse is treated may be dictated by the cultural background. E.g. Chinese people do not hug.

75. Likewise speech patterns may also be influenced by the culture of the couple.

76. The couple who are dedicated to setting their own cultural standard for their marriage will be successful.

77. Setting boundaries are essential prerequisites for ensuring success in the cross-cultural home.

78. Cross-cultural marriages can be complex if entered into by the immature.

79. Choices and decisions regarding the home base may have to be agreed. E.g. A spouse may end up having to live in the culture of the other.

80. Make sure you know what their commitment is to the sanctity of marriage.

81. Recognise the fact that all cultures are adequate for their situation.

And Ruth said, Intreat me not to leave thee, or to return from following after thee: for whither thou goest, I will go; and where thou lodgest, I will lodge: thy people shall be my people, and thy God my God: Where thou diest, will I die, and there will I be buried: the LORD do so to me, and more also, if ought but death part thee and me.
Ruth 1:16-17 (KJV)

82. Do not insist on your spouse becoming like his or her gender would have been in your culture.

83. Know the structure of hierarchy, i.e. Patriarchal, Matriarchal.

There is the tendency to think that all cultures have the same hierarchy of leadership. There are societies where the mother figure in the greater family, gives the whole family leadership. That is a matriarchal society. And the ones in which the great-uncle takes the leadership - The *Avuncular* Society. It is necessary to know the structure of leadership in the family of your future spouse, so that you do not insult what they hold in high regard.

84. Agreement should include what to eat.

85. Those who live or meet in a neutral culture must face the reality of the difference.

86. Racial and cultural jokes may cost your relationship the capacity to be deep.

87. There may be occasions when a second language has to be spoken, do not take it personal.

88. Cultural oddities should be discussed before they cause offence

- Some remove shoes at the door.
- Wives carrying stuff to follow husbands.

89. In-laws must not be allowed to belittle the other spouse's culture.

90. Be sure your spouse's culture has eradicated the practice of transferring the responsibility of the surviving spouse to their relations for raising children.

Cross cultural marriages are not for those who are not open to new things. You should not put upon yourself to learning alone, be ready to also change certain world views.

91. Possible prejudices held must be discussed before any cross-racial marriage.

92. Cross-racial couples must prepare to educate their children on the values and importance of their dual culture before any identity crisis.

93. Where there is constant conflict of cultures, wisdom must prevail.

94. Current upheavals around the world have increased the chances of cross-cultural marriage.

95. The persons most likely to go into cross-cultural marriages are people who are second or third generation immigrants.

96. Cross-cultural marriage is for believers whose biblical world-view is paramount and superceding to other world views.

97. Cross-cultural marriage has increased because of the redirection in the power of the extended family.

98. Before you go into cross-cultural marriage you must rise above your cultures and adjust one to another.

99. You must be ready to adapt to each other's cultures.

100. You must be ready to be teachable.

101. The Bible says to treat each other with honour.

102. You must never think one culture is superior to another.

103. Recognise the fact that there is no uncivilised culture.

All cultures have enough tools, linguistics, methodology, music and other expressions to be civilised within their system. It is only when they are compared to another culture that they may be regarded to be otherwise.

43
truths about
divorce
and
re-marriage

104. Recognise that any which way it takes place - God hates divorce because it is an act of unfaithfulness to the solemnness of the covenant which two partners have come into before God.

He that diggeth a pit shall fall into it; and whoso breaketh an hedge,
a serpent shall bite him.
Ecclesiastes 10:8 (KJV)

105. Divorce has cumulative consequences that are harmful to all involved - the partners, their children and possibly relations.

For the LORD, the God of Israel, saith that he hateth putting away:
for one covereth violence with his garment, saith the LORD of hosts:
therefore take heed to your spirit, that ye deal not treacherously.
Malachi 2:16 (KJV)

Divorce was only permitted in Scripture to accommodate the sinfulness of man. It may seem an easy option, but it has more to it than meets the eye. Though people may be divorced they never really leave one another, at least the memory.

106. Divorce was only in Scripture to protect the one member of the relationship who was a faithful partner, who was being oppressed by the breaking of the covenant by the other partner, and put in a position where they could no longer fulfil the covenant duties they were committed to fulfil.

107. Jesus made it clear that divorce was only permitted because of the hardness of human hearts as exhibited by the Children of Israel.

He saith unto them, Moses because of the hardness of your
hearts suffered you to put away your wives: but from the beginning
it was not so.
Matthew 19:8 (KJV)

God's ideal is still the same, that men and women who come
together in relationship should live together until 'death do
them part'.

The wife is bound by the law as long as her husband liveth;
but if her husband be dead, she is at liberty to be married to whom
she will; only in the Lord.
1 Corinthians 7:39 (KJV)

108. The teaching of Christ clearly shows us that divorce was an attempt by God to accommodate the sinfulness of man - which violates God's original intention which is - intimacy, unity, permanence and procreation.

Matthew 19:3-9 (KJV)

Therefore shall a man leave his father and his mother, and shall cleave
unto his wife: and they shall be one flesh.
Genesis 2:24 (KJV)

109. Jesus' exposition on the subject in Matthew 19:3 when He said "For any cause at all" is an attempt to correct the Jews misconception that they divorce one another for any reason they like.

The Pharisees also came unto him, tempting him, and saying unto him,
Is it lawful for a man to put away his wife for every cause?
Matthew 19:3 (KJV)

It was also to show them the gravity of pursuing divorce,
outside of the reasons which the scriptures give.

110. Divorce is a concession from the faithful partner to the disobedience of the other partner in his or her relationship to God - so that the faithful partner is not kept in bondage and made to suffer the consequence and intolerable situation created by the unfaithful.

But I say unto you, That whosoever shall put away his wife, saving for the cause of fornication, causeth her to commit adultery: and whosoever shall marry her that is divorced committeth adultery.
Matthew 5:32 (KJV)

And I say unto you, Whosoever shall put away his wife, except it be for fornication, and shall marry another, committeth adultery: and whoso marrieth her which is put away doth commit adultery.
Matthew 19:9 (KJV)

Isaiah 7:12-15 (KJV)

111. The believer is taught not to consider divorce, except in extreme circumstances.

The circumstances are not enough, there must be enough Scriptural grounds and pastoral insight sought.

112. The believer is not to consider divorce unless other options, eg. reconciliation are now almost impossible, and the pursuit of it must be with a certain degree of reluctance.

It is not Scriptural for any church, organisation, ministry or group of people to give the impression that all you need to divorce your spouse is a mere dislike.

113. In the case of adultery, desertion or divorce - the faithful partner in such a relationship must recognise their responsibility to forgive the offending - and make attempts to reconcile with the unfaithful.

Take heed to yourselves: If thy brother trespass against thee, rebuke him; and if he repent, forgive him. And if he trespass against thee seven times in a day, and seven times in a day turn again to thee, saying, I repent; thou shalt forgive him.
Luke 17:3-4 (KJV)
And be ye kind one to another, tenderhearted, forgiving one another, even as God for Christ's sake hath forgiven you.
Ephesians 4:32 (KJV)

114. A leader who has been previously divorced should not be rushed into the hierarchies of leadership until his present relationship reflects the new quality of life, he claims to possess.

The previous reputation of his relationship must also be taken into consideration before levels of leadership are allowed for such a person.

A bishop then must be blameless, the husband of one wife, vigilant, sober, of good behaviour, given to hospitality, apt to teach;
1 Timothy 3:2 (KJV)

115. God's Word commands us to forgive one another - the believer must pursue this at all times.

So likewise shall my heavenly Father do also unto you, if ye from your hearts forgive not every one his brother their
trespasses.
Matthew 18:35 (KJV)

Take heed to yourselves: If thy brother trespass against thee, rebuke him; and if he repent, forgive him. And if he trespass against thee seven times in a day, and seven times in a day turn again to thee, saying, I repent; thou shalt forgive him.
Luke 17:3-4 (KJV)

116. The pursuit of forgiveness is also applicable in the case of divorce or other extreme marital issues - as long as the offender has sought for forgiveness and has shown the fruit of repentance.

The person who cannot forgive has burnt the bridge upon which they may have to travel one day. Forgiveness following a repentance helps to define the difference between the person who falls into sin, and the one who lives in it.

117. The number one ground mentioned in Scripture for divorce is unrepentant sexual sin - not just sexual sin.

And he saith unto them, Whosoever shall put away his wife, and marry another, committeth adultery against her. And if a woman shall put away her husband, and be married to another, she committeth adultery.
Mark 10:11-12 (KJV)

118. The pursuit of reconciliation must be done wholeheartedly, prayerfully, biblically with counselling and in submission to every method of discipline initiated by the local church.

The faithful person who is in the process of reconciling must recognise that forgiveness and reconciliation are linked in the Scriptures - therefore you could not assume forgiving without wanting to reconcile. The forgiveness given must reflect God's forgiveness.

Matthew 5:23-24 (KJV); Matthew 18:15 (KJV)
Ephesians 4:32 (KJV); Colossians 3:13 (KJV)

119. God also allows divorce where there is no way for the faithful partner to fulfil the covenant obligations of companionship and sexual oneness.

The complications of modernity are making certain people to make their spouses have difficulty in fulfilling their marriage vows. Some for economic convenience would migrate elsewhere. And because they are working they stay away from their spouse for a lengthy period. Sometimes for as long as ten years. In such cases the person in question has made the marriage vow difficult for their spouse to fulfill.

120. In a case where a sinning partner makes attempt to renew the covenant, the faithful partner must make attempt to make it happen.

Any attempt to scuttle a genuine attempt to reconcile would also be unfaithfulness to the covenant shared. Jesus did not leave us in doubt as to what demands marriage may put on us. Reconciliation with estranged spouses is not as easy as other matters, but the Scriptures must be obeyed.

121. Initiating a divorce procedure at a time when reconciliation is sought by the unfaithful partner - is the breaking of the covenant vows which the faithful is committed to.

Then came Peter to him, and said, Lord, how oft shall my brother sin against me, and I forgive him? till seven times? Jesus saith unto him, I say not unto thee, Until seven times: but, Until seventy times seven.
Matthew 18:21-22 (KJV)

122. Sexual sin is not an automatic cancellation of a marriage bond - it is the cause and a ground for such break-up.

But I say unto you, That whosoever shall put away his wife, saving for the cause of fornication, causeth her to commit adultery: and whosoever shall marry her that is divorced committeth adultery.

Matthew 5:32 (KJV)

It strains a marriage and could cause the final divorcing, but it does not mean that the marriage no longer exists.

123. In Matthew 5:32; 19:19 - the word Jesus used was *pornea* or any form of sexual sin - therefore the strongest Biblical ground for divorce will be unrepentant sexual sin or desertion by an unbeliever.

But I say unto you, That whosoever shall put away his wife, saving for the cause of fornication, causeth her to commit adultery: and whosoever shall marry her that is divorced committeth adultery.

Matthew 5:32 (KJV)

And I say unto you, Whosoever shall put away his wife, except it be for fornication, and shall marry another, committeth adultery: and whoso marrieth her which is put away doth commit adultery.

Matthew 19:9 (KJV)

Pornea will cover every form of sexual sin which a spouse does not repent of - adultery, homosexuality, bestiality, incest, etc.

124. Re-marriage is possible for the one who is faithful in a relationship - if the divorce was on Biblical grounds.

A brief recap on possible grounds for re-marriage would be the case where the other person continues to live in adultery, abuses against one's spouse that are clearly a violation of the Scriptures and their right as humans, and the case where one's spouse has made it difficult for covenant responsibilities to be fulfilled.

125. When one partner forsakes the unity, intimacy and oneness of a marriage - they make it difficult for the faithful to fulfil their obligation and covenant responsibilities.

Therefore shall a man leave his father and his mother, and shall cleave unto his wife: and they shall be one flesh.

Genesis 2:24 (KJV)

Now concerning the things whereof ye wrote unto me: It is good for a man not to touch a woman. Nevertheless, to avoid fornication, let every man have his own wife, and let every woman have her own husband. Let the husband render unto the wife due benevolence: and likewise also the wife unto the husband. The wife hath not power of her own body, but the husband: and likewise also the husband hath not power of his own body, but the wife. Defraud ye not one the other, except it be with consent for a time, that ye may give yourselves to fasting and prayer; and come together again, that Satan tempt you not for your incontinency.

1 Corinthians 7:1-5 (KJV)

126. In the extreme cases where peace is an answer - where there has been abuse, misuse, etc, divorce is actually more preferable in such situations - since peace cannot be maintained if there is no divorce .

But if the unbelieving depart, let him depart. A brother or a sister is not under bondage in such cases: but God hath called us to peace.

1 Corinthians 7:15 (KJV)

127. When an unbelieving mate does not desire to live with the believer, divorce becomes permitted for the believing spouse, especially because of the believer's Christian testimony.

But to the rest speak I, not the Lord: If any brother hath a wife that believeth not, and she be pleased to dwell with him, let him not put her away. And the woman which hath an husband that believeth not, and if he be pleased to dwell with her, let her not leave him. For the unbelieving husband is sanctified by the wife, and the unbelieving wife is sanctified by the husband: else were your children unclean; but now are they holy. But if the unbelieving depart, let him depart. A brother or a sister is not under bondage in such cases: but God hath called us to peace.

1 Corinthians 7:12-15 (KJV)

128 There is a strong word against divorce that is not on Biblical grounds - where such takes place, the man or woman who marries a divorcee are themselves adulterers.

And if a woman shall put away her husband, and be married to
another, she committeth adultery.
Mark 10:12 (KJV)

129. In some cases an unbelieving partner may have left the home because of certain reasons; refusal to file for divorce, lifestyle, irresponsibility, avoiding monetary obligations, avoiding certain commitments.

In such a case the believer has been left in an intolerable
situation to fulfil the legal and moral obligation. In such a case
the brother or sister is not under bondage.

But if the unbelieving depart, let him depart. A brother or a sister is not
under bondage in such cases: but God hath called us to peace.
1 Corinthians 7:15 (KJV)

In other words they no longer need to remain married, divorce
becomes acceptable without fearing the displeasure of God
because they have been put in a situation where they cannot
keep obligations which marriage has drawn them into.

130. Believers who marry on unbiblical grounds have openly rejected the Word of God and therefore should be disciplined in one form or another.

The discipline of the believer who has openly rejected the Bible's standard must itself be open and clear to all members. The purpose must be to send a message that the Church does not intend to tolerate any unbiblical action. The discipline must convey the gravity with which the church takes the action of such a believer.

131. There are many flimsy reasons and grounds which people give for divorce. This would lead to sinning against God and their partners, and the Scriptures says where such takes place, such a person must remain unmarried or else be reconciled to their spouse.

And unto the married I command, yet not I, but the Lord, Let not the wife depart from her husband: But and if she depart, let her remain unmarried, or be reconciled to her husband: and let not the husband put away his wife.
1 Corinthians 7:10-11 (KJV)

132. People who attain an unbiblical divorce and remarry must be made to understand they are living in a state of adultery - since God does not recognise the validity of their divorce.

But I say unto you, That whosoever shall put away his wife, saving for the cause of fornication, causeth her to commit adultery: and whosoever shall marry her that is divorced committeth adultery.
Matthew 5:32 (KJV)

And if a woman shall put away her husband, and be married to another, she committeth adultery.
Mark 10:12 (KJV)

133. If a born-again Christian breaks their marriage covenant and refuses to repent, and if they also refuse to submit to the discipline of the church, the Scriptures instruct that we treat such as an unsaved person - *1 Corinthians 5:1-13*.

1 Corinthians 5:1-13 (KJV)

134. Enough time should be allowed for an unsaved spouse, or an unfaithful spouse to change their mind and return - possibly because of the discipline they have been put under.

135. For divorced single persons, the local church must treat each case on its own merit, studying carefully if the situation has been such that it biblically allows the single person to re-marry.

The subject of separation, divorce and re-marriage is complicated, and because of our humanity has a certain unique touch per case. It is important that each case be dealt with, taking into account, the setting, circumstance, stand and spiritual understanding of the people in question. While there is no category for wrong or sin, the divorce of a person in leadership, and possible re-marriage should require more care and caution than the average person in the local church.

...... For unto whomsoever much is given, of him shall be much required: and to whom men have committed much, of him they will ask the more.
Luke 12:48b (KJV)

136. The church should study each case on its own merit. It should understand whether the two persons or the one person known in church was married at the time and were legitimately born-again, or if it was when they were not saved and therefore did not know the biblical principles to the which they should have submitted.

1 Corinthians 7:17-24 (KJV)

137. In the case where a partner who is estranged has moved to another fellowship, refusing to submit to discipline, the church should consider if such a Christian should be regarded as an unbeliever, because of his continuous disobedience to discipline and the Word of God.

But if the unbelieving depart, let him depart. A brother or a sister is not under bondage in such cases: but God hath called us to peace.

1 Corinthians 7:15 (KJV)

Be ye not unequally yoked together with unbelievers: for what fellowship hath righteousness with unrighteousness? and what communion hath light with darkness?

2 Corinthians 6:14 (KJV)

138. The state of a person at the time they got born again, would influence what they do on the subject of marriage, divorce and relationships.

People who have been bruised in relationships, consider another one too hot to handle. It is important for the Christian who has just been born-again to develop a relationship with God. Following that they can then think of their relationship with the opposite sex.

139 Any believer who is divorced and seems to not be clear on their case should humbly seek the Lord and the leadership of the local church in which they belong for a clear ruling on their matter. Trusting that the leadership they have submitted to will be matured enough.

Verily I say unto you, Whatsoever ye shall bind on earth shall be bound in heaven: and whatsoever ye shall loose on earth shall be loosed in heaven.
Matthew 18:18 (KJV)

140. In the case where divorce took place not on Biblical grounds. For the guilty partner - if they repent, the grace of God becomes operative and must therefore seek reconciliation according to 1 Corinthians 7:11.

But and if she depart, let her remain unmarried, or be reconciled to her husband: and let not the husband put away his wife.
1 Corinthians 7:11 (KJV)

141. If they were born again while they were divorced and their previous spouse is unsaved, they could not now seek reconciliation because it would mean getting married to an unbeliever.

Rather they are free to marry a believer.

The wife is bound by the law as long as her husband liveth; but if her husband be dead, she is at liberty to be married to whom she will; only in the Lord.
1 Corinthians 7:39 (KJV)

Be ye not unequally yoked together with unbelievers: for what fellowship hath righteousness with unrighteousness? and what communion hath light with darkness?
2 Corinthians 6:14 (KJV)

142. When a person gets saved they begin a new life. At such time the believer has a responsibility to obey God and to follow His revealed will.

At such times what they know about marriage and divorce from the point of their salvation would hold on their life.

Therefore if any man be in Christ, he is a new creature: old things are passed away; behold, all things are become new.
2 Corinthians 5:17 (KJV)

There are individuals whom before their salvation have had a lifestyle entangled in several relationships. We must recognise the newness of life which they have in Christ. Failure to apply the Scriptures effectively in this area have made people to sometimes demand that a man or woman go back to a spouse who has left them many years ago or in some cases has already been re-married. The new Christian is told in such situations to keep waiting for their previous spouse's relationship to break down, so they can now go into marriage. This cannot work and where it does not, the Christian becomes frustrated.

143. The purity, sanctity, and identity of marriage must be exemplified and practiced by the leadership of the local church as a deterrent to further divorces.

A bishop then must be blameless, the husband of one wife, vigilant, sober, of good behaviour, given to hospitality, apt to teach; Let the deacons be the husbands of one wife, ruling their children and their own houses well.

1 Timothy 3:2,12 (KJV)

144. Church leadership requires a high standard of qualification, nonetheless it does not preclude formally divorced people who have taken proper steps, since other qualifications mentioned for getting marriage right, may have been met by such persons.

Furthermore the qualities required in monogamy are qualities which are currently characterised in a person's life.

145. Where a believer obtains a divorce on grounds that are not Biblical and remarries, he is guilty of adultery until he confesses that sin and asks for God's forgiveness.

And he saith unto them, Whosoever shall put away his wife, and marry another, committeth adultery against her. And if a woman shall put away her husband, and be married to another, she committeth adultery.
Mark 10:11-12 (KJV)

God forgives sin immediately and where repentance takes place, we cannot hold a person anymore to the sin which they have confessed. At such times the person should continue in her current marriage, but according to Biblical principles. To obtain a second divorce would disobey scriptures according to Deuteronomy 24:1-4

When a man hath taken a wife, and married her, and it come to pass that she find no favour in his eyes, because he hath found some uncleanness in her: then let him write her a bill of divorcement, and give it in her hand, and send her out of his house. And when she is departed out of his house, she may go and be another man's wife. And if the latter husband hate her, and write her a bill of divorcement, and giveth it in her hand, and sendeth her out of his house; or if the latter husband die, which took her to be his wife; Her former husband, which sent her away, may not take her again to be his wife, after that she is defiled; for that is abomination before the LORD: and thou shalt not cause the land to sin, which the LORD thy God giveth thee for an inheritance.
Deuteronomy 24:1-4 (KJV)

146. Where reconciliation is not possible and the former spouse is an unbeliever or is re-married, then the forgiven believer could pursue a new relationship - but with the direction and guidance of the leadership of the local church where they belong.

The church has a responsibility of researching and doing what is right and appropriate on this matter. Because of its nature as a hospital of the soul, it will attract people who, for example at the age of thirty have already been in three marriages. They probably do not know where the first person they ever married is, and do not have an address of the third. To ask them to go back to a previous spouse, will mean to expose them to the lifestyle from which they have been rescued.

36 questions a person should ask before they say ' I do'

147. Why do I want to get married to this person?

It is important for a single person to check what is the drive behind their making a choice of a partner. It could be desperation - they need to quickly supply a person into that area of their life, called marriage or a partner. When the single person meets whom they think they want to share the future with, decisions must be influenced therefore by the goals pre-set before meeting the person. If you have no mental picture of where you are going, anyone will seem okay.

148. Am I ready to give up some things for sake of the relationship?

The capacity to grow in life is tied to your capacity to give. Those who do not give stay small. The amazement of life is to see how you can easily be enriched by enriching others. These are habits one must form before thinking of marriage. Because marriage is all about giving and if two people are committed to giving, no-one ends up lacking. If you are not ready to give, you are not ready to marry. A statement in the marriage vow says "And with all my worldly goods, I thee endow".

149. Am I ready for marriage spiritually, emotionally and physically?

Marriage is a relationship of two equals, where one person is ordained by God to be the head. The readiness of the two people to share their lives cannot be underplayed. Emotional readiness is the ability to be able to express yourselves emotionally without feeling guilty, and without being dictated to by other people. Spiritual readiness is your ability to bring a clear and qualitative relationship with God into this marriage, so that it is not totally physical but built on the foundation of truth and the spiritual. Physical readiness is the ability to have dealt with all inhibitions one has about sharing the future. To have set sexual boundaries, thereby keeping oneself pure before the day of marriage, and to have dealt with any fears one has when it comes to sexual relationships. It also means that you are physically attracted, yet in a healthy way to the person you would share the future with. Being Christian does not mean that there will not be sexual attraction.

150. Is there evidence that there is a mutual understanding of each other's vision?

Can two walk together, except they be agreed?
Amos 3:3 (KJV)

151. How understanding is my future spouse of my desires, dreams, and goals?

152. Have we spent sufficient time getting to know each other as friends?

153. How financially stable will we be?

154. How do family, friends and mentors react to my future spouse?

155. How much do I really know about my future spouse?

156. Am I prepared to pray for my future spouse's weaknesses and celebrate his strengths?

157. What impact will the work, ministry, vision, and goals of my future spouse have on my life?

158. How will my future spouse's family and friends impact my life?

159. Will my future spouse respect and keep to issues agreed between us?

160. What evidence do I have that my future spouse is prepared to be the priest, provider and protector of the home?

161. How does my future spouse view marriage?

162. How committed is my future spouse to ensuring the marriage will work?

163. How well do we currently communicate and express our feelings, needs and wants?

164. To what lengths is my future spouse prepared to work at maintaining healthy communication?

165. Am I prepared to let go of family ties, emotionally, spiritually and physically?

166. Are you friends, apart from the marriage relationship?

167. Are you mutual mentors of each other in spiritual matters?

168. Are you proud to introduce each other to your friends?

169. Do your differences compliment one another's strengths and weaknesses?

170. Have you dealt with previous relationships that can affect the present?

171. How comfortable do I feel about the marriage counselling we have received?

172. How responsive is my future spouse to correction?

173. Am I able to disagree constructively with my future spouse without feeling bad?

174. Does my future spouse honour, esteem and encourage me?

175. Am I able to submit to my future spouse?

176. Am I proud of my future spouse's appearance, ministry, work, etc?

177. Am I prepared to follow my future spouse anywhere?

178. Am I able to respect my future spouse's decisions?

179. Am I able to take correction from my future spouse?

180. Am I prepared to spend the rest of my life with my future spouse?

181. Am I fully aware of my future spouse's medical history?

182. Am I comfortable with my future's spouse's world view?

37
ways to
recognise
your life
partner

183. Your life partner is the only right person to connect you to your destiny.

Joseph had many wrong people, but one butler to connect him to his destiny. Samson made a shipwreck of his life, because of one lady.

184. There are certain characteristics which have already come up in your spirit about your life partner - write them, read them, run with the vision!

185. Your life partner will be a person who is compatible with the goal of your future.

186. The people who come into your life help or hinder your goal. The person chosen to be your partner would help you to get to your goal fast.

187. The people who come into your life help to unlock your dreams. Some lock up your dreams and visions. The person chosen to be your partner would unlock them.

188. The first step in knowing who God has chosen for you is a personal self-recognition. You must know who you are before you know whom God has chosen for you.

And the LORD God said, It is not good that the man should be alone; I will make him an help meet for him.
Genesis 2:18 (KJV)

189. There must be a recognition that you are incomplete without God's ordained partner for your life.

190. You must recognise and respect God's choice for your life, because what you do not respect will move away from you. What you respect will come to you.
The person who does not know the purpose of a mate will abuse the one who comes to him.

191. The way to know your partner is what they are transformed into when they are in your presence. Angels or devils! Loving people or lustful people!

192. The next way to recognise your partner of the future is if they bring out the strength in you. People around you either provoke your weakness or your strength.

193. The recognition of your future partner will come in the fact that the love you have for them is void of fear. People are sometimes caught in the fear of losing the person, or being hurt in the future.

194. Your partner of the future will bring a blessing which you would miss if you were single. There is a benefit to being single, but the way to recognise your future partner is that they give you the joy of completion.

195. The next way to know your partner of the future is that they never remain the way you met them, they get better daily and confirm your conviction in marriage.

196. Your spouse of the future will satisfy your goals, vision and desires - not just stimulate your emotion. Stimulation only appeals to the physical, satisfaction goes deeper.

197. Another way to recognise whom God has sent to your life, is that they celebrate and value who you are, without trying to make you who they want you to be.

198. Your spouse of the future has points of differences, yet values certain things which you hold similarly.

199. You would recognise the person whom God has chosen for your life because they fill a void which even access to God would not take away.

And the LORD God said, It is not good that the man should be alone; I will make him an help meet for him.
Genesis 2:18 (KJV)

Adam was created by God to have connection with people, he felt alone even though he enjoyed the presence of God.

200. The person chosen for your life would celebrate your ambitions in life. The failure to know your vision and calling would also result in the failure to receive the endorsement of your future partner.

201. You would recognise your future partner by the fact that your vision does not distract or cause them to dread, but makes them desire and want to share the future with you.

Your future spouse will even be looking for ways to encourage your purpose and make it happen.

202. In the case where you have children, your future partner does not only tolerate the presence of your children, but treats them as his or hers.

203.   Your future partner will put a value to your life as Christ values the church, as the church values and submits to Christ.

A person who will not value his mother or father and honour them, may be a source of trouble for your future.

204. The first sign of trouble is a person who has developed a very bad attitude toward his parent. If he fails to honour his parent, he will not honour you.

205. One of the ways to recognise who you will share the future with is that if you are hardworking, they would be too. You cannot be an achiever and pursue a lazy bone. You cannot be an achiever and pursue a person that loves to live on welfare.

206. You would recognise the person you need to share the future with by the way they treat and relate to their superiors, their bosses, the church authorities.

207. A most outstanding sign of the person to share your future with is if he is a lover of the Word. Faithfulness begins with the person's commitment to the Word of God and the cleansing of His life with the Word of God.

208. The person you want to share your future with will prove himself by the kind of attitude he has towards money. You cannot shy away from financial matters. Ninety percent of marital conflicts are centered around money, and the man who is not a provider is worse than an infidel.

But if any provide not for his own, and specially for those of his own house, he hath denied the faith, and is worse than an infidel.
1 Timothy 5:8 (KJV)

209. You will be attracted to your future partner by the strength he or she has. That strength may be in their ability to focus on you and help you to achieve what God has called you to do. Ruth helped Naomi and Naomi told Ruth when to talk to Boaz.

210. The person you will share the future with, will be marked by his attitude and ability to show mercy. Watch out for how he treats people in problems, and people who face needs. How he forgives, and receives forgiveness himself.

211. You would recognise the person whom God has chosen for you by how he chooses to shun unrighteousness and live right.

212. Your future spouse will be marked out by the problems he has dedicated himself to solve for others. You will see who surrounds him, the people he has brought joy to, and those he has brought hope to.

213. The person who has been marked to be your partner will be recognised by the fact that he goes all out to solve problems for you.

214. Those ordained to share the future with you, will bring joy into your life.

Moments of disagreement will Come

215. The person who has been ordained to be your future partner, will be recognised by the fact that he encourages a warm relationship between him and your relations and encourages the continuity of your relationship with your relations.

216. The person you would share the future with is marked out by his ability to not be snowed under every challenge that comes, but on top of it. You cannot afford a person you keep raising all the time.

217. Your partner of the future will stand out by the fact that in spite of the knowledge of your past, does not reject you, but is willing to go all the way with you.

218. You would discern the person you are called to share the future with by the mentors he has chosen for his life. To know what Joshua would turn out to be, we see what Moses became. To try to see into the future of Elisha, we see what Elijah became. To grasp Esther's future, all we need is Mordecai's present. A man's heroes are a picture of his own future.

219. Open yourself to God's method for communicating His mind to His people. The primary source of God communicating His mind to His people is His Word, that is the final and infallible source for knowing the mind of God. Other than that you can receive by word of knowledge, word of wisdom, dreams, trance, a silent witness in your spirit that God had spoken.

25
truths
about
co-habitation

220. Do not get into the living together thing. "Because it is popular does not mean it is God".

A recent US poll showed that sixty-six percent of young people aged eighteen to thirty-two believed you should first live together before you get married. (*NBC Newspoll of 1996/Spin Magazine*). Yet because a thing is popular does not mean it is right or workable. Scripturally it does not tally with God's Word, and experientially it leaves more people bruised.

221. You cannot say because there is a multiplication of wrong it makes it right. No, the standard of God stands sure.

The majority of people who live together would argue that it helps them to prove the depths of their love before they eventually get married. It helps them to manage their finances and not waste money on their way to getting married in the future. It must have been logical for the people in the days of Noah to not go into the Ark, after all they had never seen the rain fall before. But when the rain began to fall, and the consequences of their disobedience was manifest, they must have been regretful.

222. To get it right, you have to do it God's way. Doing God's will may be painful now but it pays later.

Celibacy before marriage may not be practical today, but what it does is help the single person develop character and the ability to restrain themselves. The practice of self-control has essentially become strange to a generation that is into instant gratification. Sexual restraint and avoiding living together helps you to build the ability to keep trusting one another, and a healthy foundation for joy in the future. Where the relationship does not continue, you are able to look at each other eyeball to eyeball without any sense of guilt, and yet belong in the same local church or in the neighbourhood.

223. Living together pulls you away from the Lord.

Marriage is honourable in all, and the bed undefiled: but whoremongers and adulterers God will judge.
Hebrews 13:4 (KJV)

224. Living together clouds your opinion of the partner.

Beneath the smiles and the impressions of joy projected by people who are living together, is a life of worry. Because one person may say it is over, it might result in pregnancies, or the other person might contact some kind of venereal disease.

225. Co-habiting is a major reason for a lot of heartbreaks.

The ideal for all people is to make a commitment to marriage. The possibilities are there that one person in a co-habiting relationship prefers immediate marriage, but the other person is not giving them the opportunity. This lack of commitment is likely to continue if they eventually get marriage. A person who is unable to make a commitment before marriage and while living together, because he or she cannot delay gratification, is likely to want to continue to not delay gratification when the occasion presents itself of his now married life.

226. Co-habiting may result in unwanted pregnancy.

The majority of men who co-habit do it for easy sex. Pregnancy would be seen as the woman's problem, she would have to sort it out herself. Where children are born, the problem gets complicated because there is no commitment to one another.

227. It is likely to hurt the children caught up in this mess.

Children born out of wedlock go through bouts of rejection and low self-esteem, and eventual expression of rebellion. The ones born out of blended relationships - where the man or the woman brought children into the relationship and yet are not married, but are only living together have their life even more complicated because of the uncertainty looming over the head. The man is in the relationship for the sex, the woman is in the relationship hoping that marriage would take place. Each is tiptoeing around the other because it could fall apart. While the parents have developed enough anti-histamine to handle continuous emotional let downs. The children are unprepared for this, it launches them on the sea of their own emotional baggages.

228. It is likely to eventually destroy the relationship.

With marriage on the mind of the woman and free sex on the mind of the man. A woman in the living together thing, who has done everything she thinks she should do; treat him right, cook his food and take care of his house, then finds that he is not prepared to pay her services of supplying free sex will suddenly wake up to see the relationship has to be over.

229. Being with this person may be a hindrance to meeting the right person.

The majority of those who go into co-habitation quote love as their motive, but beneath it is likely to be the fear of divorce, and therefore trying the person they want to live with, thinking that might protect them from having to break up again. It is also informed by the fear of missing their chance and not meeting the right person. If anything co-habitation delays the chance to meet the right person, it further complicates ones life story and reduces all the opportunities for a truly happy married life in the future.

230. It will hinder your marital hopes and dreams.

231. Everyone you co-habit with leaves a bit of themselves with you.

Co-habitation is like lying with a dog and coming up with fleas. It is not possible to walk away from it as easily as people think. It certainly would feel like having gone through a divorce. All divorced persons may walk away from the person, but there is a certain remembrance with whom they are in the relationship. The mental torture, the physical abuse, the things they did together or did not do together stays with them as they move into another co-habitation. They do the same thing divorced people do, until they are matured, which is comparing this new partner with the old.

232. You cannot feel totally secure in the relationship.

Co-habitees go into it for security, but once they are in they find that it is the most insecure relationship. Because it lacks all the elements of security in marriage. There is no commitment from the other person. You cannot trust whatever they say, you are forever vulnerable because somebody else might show up in the picture. You cannot guarantee that when you get home the other person will be there, and you might one day find you have been living with an illusion of who the person really is.

233. Male and female reasons for co-habitation are often different.

The majority of men are in co-habitation for convenient sexual relationships. It is like getting a free supply of what one should pay a price for. Most women in a situation of co-habitation, are in it with the hopes that marriage would take place one day. They are prepared to do everything and put on a facade to impress the man to give them a ring. They believe if they treat him right; cook his food, take care of his children, he will see them as the right person. The worst situation is to be co-habiting with a commitment phobic. He is not likely to ever give the woman what she wants, no matter what price she paid.

234. If you marry, the unhealthy dynamic in that relationship will stay.

235. The price of heartbreak is more than the challenge of celibacy.

Living together gives a temporary satisfaction to a permanent hunger. But when that supply is abruptly taken away or broken, the challenge it leaves is even worst than being alone in the first place. Because along with being alone, you are also left with bad memories. It is a game of chance, and results have shown high incidences of depression for women who have co-habited than for married or un-married women.

236. Where children are involved, they cannot be guaranteed a stable home.

Children need a stable home in order to have a healthy development. The complications of relationships today have redefined the setting in which many children have been raised. But probably the worst is where children raised in a home where the parents are co-habiting. The same fear the parents lived with, the man under the fear that his supply of sex will stop, the woman under the fear that she might not get the marriage she wanted, but even then, it is more complicated with the children.

237. Children from previous relationships can be badly hurt.

There is no commitment to their natural parent from the person with whom he or she co-habits. Secondly, if the parent is into the habit of co-habiting, they would know several step-fathers and mothers. Where one of the co-habitants threatens to leave, or manipulates the situation, children who are in this relationship who are co-dependents suffer the most. In every bad relationship co-dependents suffer more because they do not get any gratification. At least the mother is getting some level of emotional commitment, the man is getting whatever motivates him to be in the relationship, while the children pick the pieces.

238. People living together cannot claim married couple's tax allowance.

Unless the law changes, people in co-habitation are regarded as two singles, and therefore not entitled to married couples allowance.

239. Married people have obligations to maintain the other person despite separation, no law binds co-habitants.

240. Gifts between husband and wife may be free from capital tax gains, but not with co-habitants.

241. Your co-habitant cannot insure your life, married people can.

242. If a married person dies intestate, most of his or her estate goes to a spouse, but a co-habitant is not legally entitled to anything.

Where a people have co-habited and a spouse dies, the family of the deceased may step in and claim all that belongs to him or her and if it cannot be traced, it may be passed on as the government pleases.

243. Widows may claim Widowed Mother's allowance. Bereaved co-habitants cannot claim extra state benefit.

244. Statistics show that the divorce rate is high among co-habitants.

Nine in ten marriages of those who started by co-habiting does not work. The possible reason is because the excitement of marriage has dissipated with the years, when the relationship was built on suspicions, fears and lack of trust.